DJUSI

Public Sch

ˀrary Protection Act 1998

COUNTDOWN TO SPACE

GUS GRISSOM
A Space Biography

Carmen Bredeson

Series Advisor:
John E. McLeaish
Chief, Public Information Office, retired,
NASA Johnson Space Center

Enslow Publishers, Inc.

40 Industrial Road	PO Box 38
Box 398	Aldershot
Berkeley Heights, NJ 07922	Hants GU12 6BP
USA	UK

http://www.enslow.com

Library of Congress Cataloging-in-Publication Data

Bredeson, Carmen
  Gus Grissom: a space biography / Carmen Bredeson.
    p. cm. — (Countdown to space)
  Includes bibliographical references (p.) and index.
  Summary: A biography of one of America's first seven astronauts, focusing on the training and career of Gus Grissom, who died in a fire aboard Apollo 1 in 1967.
  ISBN 0-89490-974-6
  1. Grissom, Virgil I.—Juvenile literature. 2. Astronauts—United States—Biography—Juvenile literature. [1. Grissom, Virgil I. 2. Astronauts.]
I. Title. II. Series.
TL789.85.G7B74   1998
629.45' 0092—dc21
  [B]   97-21343
                                                  CIP
                                                   AC

Printed in the United States of America

10 9 8 7 6 5 4 3

Illustration Credits: National Aeronautics and Space Administration (NASA), pp. 4, 6, 9, 12, 15, 16, 19, 20, 22, 24, 25, 27, 28, 30, 33, 34, 36, 39.

Cover Illustration: National Aeronautics and Space Administration (NASA) (foreground); Raghvendra Sahai and John Trauger (JPL), the WFPC2 science team, NASA, and AURA/STSCI (background).

CONTENTS

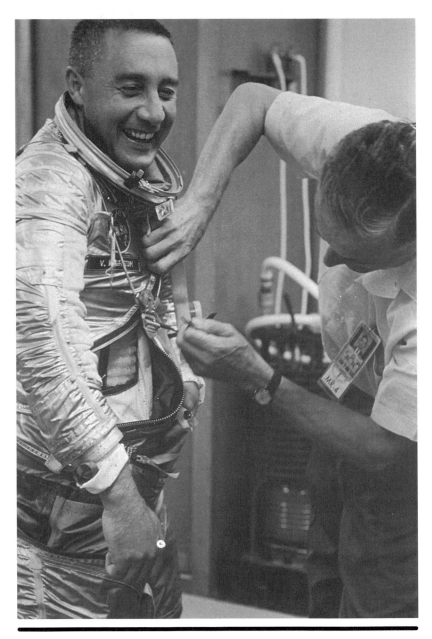

Gus Grissom is in good spirits as suit specialist Joe W. Schmidt helps him dress for his fifteen minutes in space.

1

Waiting for Liftoff

Early on the morning of July 21, 1961, technicians helped Gus Grissom pull a silver-colored spacesuit onto his stocky body. The astronaut then wiggled his way into a small opening in the cabin of his spacecraft, *Liberty Bell 7*. After strapping himself into a reclining seat, Grissom could do little except lie and wait for the countdown to begin. His spaceflight, only the second one tried by the United States, was about to begin.

As Grissom waited for liftoff, millions of Americans stayed tuned to live news broadcasts. Many experimental rockets had blown up in the past. Would the Mercury-Redstone rocket under *Liberty Bell 7* also explode and end the life of thirty-five-year-old Gus Grissom? His flight was scheduled to last only about

fifteen minutes. Those few minutes were critical though. A fatality at this point would put the brakes on the United States space program.

Finally, after delays of more than three hours, *Liberty Bell 7* blasted off, trailing rivers of yellow and white flames in its wake. Eighty million Americans followed the historic launch on television and radio. In Newport News, Virginia, Gus Grissom's wife, Betty, and their sons, seven-year-old Mark and ten-year-old Scott, were also glued to the television. As the capsule carrying Grissom rose higher and higher in the sky, Scott clapped his hands and whistled.[1]

At 141 seconds into the

Gus Grissom takes off atop a Mercury-Redstone rocket on July 21, 1961. It was only the second United States manned mission into space.

historic flight, *Liberty Bell 7* separated from its Mercury-Redstone booster rocket. Gus Grissom radioed to Alan Shepard, who was in charge of ground communication with the spacecraft:

GRISSOM: This is *Liberty Bell 7.*

SHEPARD: Loud and clear.

GRISSOM: It is a nice ride up to now.[2]

During Grissom's flight, he performed several maneuvers with the spacecraft. He reported back to Shepard:

GRISSOM: Having a little bit of trouble with manual control.

SHEPARD: Roger.

GRISSOM: If I can get stabilized, all axes are working all right.

SHEPARD: Roger. Understand manual control is good.

GRISSOM: Roger. Sort of sluggish, more than I expected.[3]

There was not time for much maneuvering during the fifteen-minute, thirty-seven-second flight. *Liberty Bell 7* climbed 118 miles into the sky and traveled at a maximum speed of 5,280 miles per hour, but did not go into orbit. Back on the ground, National Aeronautics and Space Administration (NASA) engineers and technicians nervously watched their instruments.

As the spacecraft began its journey back to Earth, an orange and white parachute deployed to help slow its speed. *Liberty Bell 7* splashed down in the Atlantic Ocean, just three miles from the intended target. Helicopters from the recovery ship, U.S.S. *Randolph*, were soon hovering over the capsule as it bobbed in the water.

Inside *Liberty Bell 7*, Gus Grissom needed a little more time to finish checking his instruments. He radioed to the helicopter above him, "Give me three or four more minutes. I will be ready for you."[4] Grissom also had to cut the straps that held him in the chair, take off his helmet, and remove the safety release on the hatch door.

Before he could finish his work, the small explosive bolts that were set to remove the hatch cover went off prematurely. Grissom later said, "I was sitting there minding my own business when—*pow!*—I saw blue sky. The biggest shock of the whole day was seeing that door blow off."[5]

As gallons of saltwater poured through the hatch, Grissom yanked his helmet off and struggled to get out of the capsule. He scrambled to the rim of the opening, fell into the ocean, and swam for his life. The downdraft from the helicopter rotor blades pushed Grissom lower and lower in the water. To make matters worse, his suit was filling up and pulling him down.

While one helicopter hovered over Grissom, another

Bye-bye Liberty Bell! *The water-filled capsule was too heavy for the helicopter to lift.*

one successfully hooked *Liberty Bell 7*. As it tried to lift the capsule, the aircraft's engine began to overheat. The weight of the water-filled capsule was too much for the engine. *Liberty Bell 7* had to be cut loose. One of the crewmen said, "Oh, my God, we lost it!"[6] The two-million-dollar spacecraft quickly sank to the bottom of the Atlantic Ocean.

Gus Grissom was also sinking lower and lower in the water. He struggled to breathe as waves washed over him. The helicopter crew tried three times to maneuver a rescue swing into position over the astronaut. Finally, on the fourth try, Grissom got a firm hold on the swing and was hauled out of the water. After he was safely aboard the rescue helicopter, Gus Grissom's helmet was recovered, floating in the water next to a fifteen-foot shark.

A waterlogged Gus Grissom was flown to the U.S.S. *Randolph,* where he was greeted by a cheering crew. Although he was shaken up by his ordeal, he was not injured. After a medical exam, Grissom had recovered enough to fly copilot on the plane that was taking him to Grand Bahama Island for debriefing. When he was later asked about his spaceflight, Gus Grissom said, "I was scared a good part of the time. But it was so fascinating, I'd recommend the trip to everybody."[7]

From Indiana to Space

Virgil "Gus" Grissom was born in Mitchell, Indiana, on April 3, 1926. His parents, Dennis and Cecile Grissom, also had two other sons and a daughter. As a child, Gus spent some of his free time making balsa wood models of airplanes. He also belonged to the Boy Scouts. Gus liked to hunt, fish, and explore the countryside around his Indiana home.

While Gus was in high school he met his future wife, Betty Moore. At the time of the couple's 1944 graduation, the United States was involved in World War II, which lasted from 1939 until 1945. Grissom joined the Army Air Corps cadet program in order to become a pilot. By the time he finished his training, the war was over and he was discharged from the service.

Gus Grissom and Betty Moore were married soon after his discharge, on July 6, 1945.

Gus Grissom worked briefly for a company in Mitchell that built school buses and then decided to attend Purdue University in West Lafayette, Indiana. He earned his degree in mechanical engineering in 1950 and then joined the Air Force. After several months of training, Lieutenant Grissom was awarded his wings in March 1951. He was then assigned to fly an F-86 as a jet fighter pilot.

One of the first assignments the new Air Force pilot

Grissom's family—sons Scott (left) and Mark (right), and wife, Betty— joins him after his trip to space.

got was duty in Korea. The Korean War (1950–1953) was raging between Communist and non-Communist groups. As part of the United States forces' effort to aid the non-Communists in South Korea, Gus Grissom flew one hundred combat missions. For his skill in battle, the aviator was awarded the Distinguished Flying Cross and two Air Medals.

After his tour of duty in Korea ended, Grissom spent several years as an Air Force flight instructor. Betty Grissom later said, "He told me that Korea was safer than teaching cadets how to fly."[1] By 1955, Grissom had attained the rank of captain and was sent to test-pilot school at Edwards Air Force Base in California. He completed that training in May 1957 and was then sent to fly experimental aircraft at Wright Patterson Air Force Base in Ohio. It was while Grissom was in Ohio that the Soviet Union launched *Sputnik 1* into orbit.

During the 1950s, both the Soviet Union and the United States had been testing rockets that were capable of sending objects into space. Progress was slow in America because many of the experimental rockets blew up. As engineers and scientists tried to figure out how to correct the problems, the Soviet Union stunned the world on October 4, 1957. Following the countdown,

"Tri" (three)
"Dva" (two)
"Odin" (one)
"Zashiganiye," (ignition), a Russian satellite blasted into space.[2]

Sputnik 1 was the size of a basketball and weighed only 184 pounds, but it was the first man-made object launched into orbit. Moscow Radio reported that the spacecraft was traveling at a speed of seventeen thousand miles an hour. It was orbiting Earth once every ninety-six minutes. Scientists and engineers in the United States were frustrated because the Soviets had beaten America into space. They quickly shifted into high gear to try and catch up.

Four months after *Sputnik 1* soared into the sky, the United States successfully launched a bullet-shaped satellite called *Explorer 1*. Finally, the United States missile program was up and running. The space race was on! The goal of both the United States and the Soviet Union was to be the first to put not just a satellite but a human being into space.

With that goal in mind, the United States Congress created NASA in 1958. One of NASA's first jobs was to find men who were willing to sit in a tiny capsule on top of a blazing rocket and be hurled into space. Each candidate for the job had to be less than five feet eleven inches tall and under forty years old. The volunteers also had to be graduates of test-pilot school and have at least fifteen hundred hours of flying time.

There were five hundred military pilots in the United States who met some of those criteria. At the time, no women were eligible to become astronauts. After the initial screening process was completed, 110

Keeping up with the Soviets: The United States launched Explorer 1 *on January 31, 1958, just a few months after* Sputnik 1.

candidates qualified for the job. Those 110 men went through extensive medical and psychological testing.

In one test, the candidate was bombarded with very high frequency sounds while strapped into a huge vibrating machine. During the test, the subject was supposed to flip switches and press buttons faster and faster. Another test involved being put into a soundproof, pitch-black, locked room for an unspecified length of time. During and after each of the tests, doctors measured blood pressure and heart rate to see how the candidates reacted to stress.

As the weeks of testing continued, more and more astronaut candidates were disqualified. Finally, only seven men remained from the original group. On April 9, 1959, a press conference was held in Washington, D.C. Standing before a crowd of reporters

The "Mercury 7": (front row, from left to right) Wally Schirra, Deke Slayton, John Glenn, Scott Carpenter; (back row) Alan Shepard, Gus Grissom, and Gordon Cooper.

and photographers, NASA Chief T. Keith Glennan introduced America's first astronauts:

Navy Lieutenant Malcolm Scott Carpenter
Air Force Captain Leroy Gordon Cooper, Jr.
Marine Lieutenant Colonel John Herschel Glenn, Jr.
Air Force Captain Virgil I. Grissom
Navy Lieutenant Commander Walter M. Schirra, Jr.
Navy Lieutenant Commander Alan B. Shepard, Jr.
Air Force Captain Donald K. Slayton

These men were to become known as the Mercury 7, after the rocket they would ride into space. Following the astronauts' introduction, the audience rose to its feet and began clapping and cheering. Questions were fired at the seven men as flashbulbs popped like firecrackers. On stage, Donald "Deke" Slayton thought, "They're applauding us like we've already done something, like we were heroes or something."[3]

Dozens of articles about the Mercury 7 appeared in newspapers and magazines, and interviews with them were aired on television and radio. The seven men, who were virtually unknown the day before, suddenly found themselves in the spotlight. They were viewed as the brave men "who would dare to ride the rockets that so often exploded in raging fireballs over Cape Canaveral."[4]

After the April 9 announcement, Gus Grissom said that sometimes he lay in bed at night thinking, "Now what in hell do I want to go up in that thing for?" His answer, "I'm a test pilot, not a philosopher. I'm too busy to worry. This is a day-to-day job for me."[5]

3

Astronaut Grissom

Once some of the excitement died down, the astronauts went to work, learning how to be spacemen. They were stationed at Langley Air Force Base in Virginia, the headquarters for NASA's Project Mercury. Most of their training took place at Cape Canaveral, Florida, however. The "Cape," as it was known, was a huge, snake-infested area covered with sand, scrub brush, and clouds of mosquitoes.

Gus Grissom and his fellow astronauts spent hours in simulators, which were replicas of the capsules that would take them into space. They practiced launch procedures and emergency drills until they knew them by heart. They went to Johnsville, Pennsylvania, to be whirled around and around in a giant centrifuge. The spinning machine copied the pressure that the men would feel during blastoff and reentry.

To introduce the men to weightlessness, they were taken up in the cargo hold of a C-131 transport plane. The plane flew up at a steep incline and then went into a sharp dive. At the top of the arc, passengers inside experienced ten to fifteen seconds of zero gravity. During their brief period of weightlessness, they floated around inside the cabin, bumping into each other and often feeling sick.

NASA technicians look on as an astronaut gets set for a dizzying experience. This centrifuge was used to imitate the pressure of blastoff and reentry.

Astronauts seem to be dancing on air inside this cargo plane. Flying in a special arc, called a Keplerian parabola, is a way to feel zero gravity within Earth's atmosphere.

When the astronauts were not being tossed around, they attended lectures on rocket propulsion, astronomy, and flight operations. Often they worked ten to twelve hours a day, practicing procedures over and over. Their training sessions did not include any flying. That was because there was little that an astronaut could do in a Mercury capsule except abort the flight in an emergency.

Gus Grissom was asked one time to compare the astronauts to other pioneers. He said, "There's a big difference between us and Columbus, Lindbergh, and the Wright Brothers. They did it themselves. We didn't think this thing up. We're just going to ride the capsule."[1] Because of their lack of control over the flight plan, the astronauts often jokingly referred to themselves as the "man in the can."

When the Mercury 7 managed to escape from the classrooms and simulators for a few hours, they found many ways to amuse themselves. Some enjoyed jogging along the shoreline on Cocoa Beach. Others bought fast cars and raced each other on the open roads at the Cape. As former test pilots, the men were used to speed and danger. Gus Grissom drove a Corvette, as did Alan Shepard and Gordon Cooper. Scott Carpenter's car was a Shelby Cobra, and Wally Schirra preferred a Maseratti. Screaming across the sand flats of the Cape in their sports cars was a way for some of the men to unwind.

As the months of training went by, decisions had to be made about who would be the first American in space. The choice was difficult for NASA officials, but they finally selected Alan Shepard to fly the first manned mission and assigned Gus Grissom to the second Mercury flight. Shepard's flight was scheduled to lift off early in May 1961.

Less than a month before Shepard's flight, Soviet cosmonaut Yuri Gagarin blasted into space aboard

Vostok 1. The first human being in space orbited Earth once before making a successful reentry and landing. After the Soviet feat, astronaut John Glenn said, "They just beat the pants off us, that's all. There's no use kidding ourselves about that. But now that the space age has begun, there's going to be plenty of work for everybody."[2]

Alan Shepard's fifteen-minute, twenty-two-second flight lifted off on May 5, 1961. *Freedom 7* did not go into orbit, but flew 116 miles up at a speed of 5,146 miles an hour. Just twenty days later, before the United States had even sent their first astronaut into orbit, President John F. Kennedy said to the members of Congress, "I believe that this nation should commit itself to achieving the goal, before this decade is out, of landing a man on the Moon and

Freedom 7 is mounted onto a Redstone rocket. Together they shot the first American into space.

returning him safely to Earth."[3] Those present in Washington jumped to their feet, applauding and shouting their approval.

Kennedy's announcement took NASA and the country by surprise. Only one American had flown in space, for just a little over fifteen minutes, and the President was talking about going to the Moon! It would take a lot of hard work and dedication to achieve that goal. Congress gave NASA $1.7 billion to get the ball rolling. The advanced technology necessary to reach the Moon had to be developed in stages, with astronaut safety always the main priority.

As NASA grew to meet Kennedy's challenge, it began to outgrow its facilities in Virginia. Since there was no room to expand at that location, a new site had to be found for NASA headquarters. Many areas of the country were examined. Finally, Houston, Texas, was selected in September 1961. The new command center for the United States space program would be built on a sixteen-hundred-acre tract that was located twenty-five miles southeast of downtown Houston.

Staff from Virginia began moving south as soon as construction started on the Manned Spacecraft Center (MSC). Located at MSC would be all of NASA's scientific, engineering, and medical departments, as well as an astronaut-training facility. In addition, all future flights would be directed from the Mission Control

A 1987 photograph shows the Johnson Space Center, formerly called the Manned Spacecraft Center, in Houston, Texas.

Center in Houston. The spacecraft would still be launched in Florida, but after liftoff the missions would be controlled from Texas.

NASA's first stage in its quest for the Moon was called Project Mercury. This stage lasted from 1958 until 1963. During those years, the space scientists and engineers accomplished several goals. They learned how to orbit a manned spacecraft and recover the capsule and astronaut. The successful flights also proved that human beings could survive and function in space.

Except for the loss of *Liberty Bell 7* when the hatch blew, the six Mercury missions went as planned. John Glenn made the third flight and became the first American to orbit Earth on February 20, 1962. During the remaining three flights, the number of orbits steadily increased. The last Mercury mission, flown by Gordon Cooper on May 15, 1963, completed twenty-two orbits of Earth.

Next on the NASA agenda was the Gemini program. First in line to fly one of these new missions was Gus Grissom.

Virgil I. "Gus" Grissom was to be the first astronaut in the Gemini program to go into space.

4

The Bridge to Apollo

Project Gemini, which was conducted between 1964 and 1966, served as a link between the Mercury and Apollo missions. The name was taken from the twin stars of the zodiac, Castor and Pollux, that are known as Gemini. Instead of the one-passenger capsules that were used during the Mercury missions, Gemini capsules held two astronauts. With the demand for astronauts growing, several additional groups of men were selected to serve as space pioneers.

The twelve Gemini flights were used as a training ground for future trips to the Moon. Astronauts would have to learn to maneuver the capsules and dock with other spacecraft. They had to practice space walks in case repairs needed to be made during missions to the

Moon. Also, longer and longer flights were scheduled to see how the human body reacted to stays in space.

After all of the preparations and training were finished, the time arrived for the first manned Gemini flight. On March 23, 1965, Gus Grissom and John Young climbed into the cabin of *Molly Brown*. Grissom nicknamed the capsule after a popular Broadway musical called *The Unsinkable Molly Brown*. Grissom said, "In naming our *Gemini 3* spacecraft, I always had in mind the unfortunate fate of my *Liberty Bell 7*, which sank like a stone when her hatch blew prematurely."[1]

When Gus Grissom roared into space aboard the eighteen-foot-long, seven-thousand-pound *Molly Brown*, he became the first person ever to fly in space twice. During the five-hour, three-orbit flight, astronauts Grissom and Young had a full schedule. The plan called for Grissom to fire a thruster rocket to slow the ship and tighten the orbit. With those maneuvers, Gus Grissom became the first American astronaut to actually "fly" a spacecraft.

Gus Grissom and John Young were selected to fly in Molly Brown, *which NASA engineers hoped would live up to its name.*

While Gus Grissom was busy with maneuvers, John Young had the job of preparing and testing some space food. The freeze-dried meals came in plastic bags and had to be mixed with water. That sounds easy, but in zero gravity liquids ball up and float away. Young had to use a squirt gun to inject water into the packages. After he mixed the dried food and water, he was supposed to taste some of it. Gus Grissom was not scheduled to eat on the five-hour, three-orbit flight.

Grissom later said, "Here I was sitting over there flying and John was fooling around with the food and all

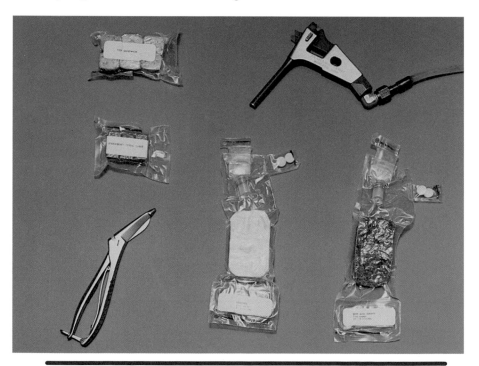

A high-tech squirt gun (upper right) was used by John Young to inject water into the packages of dehydrated food.

of a sudden he asked me if I wanted to eat."[2] Young reached into the pocket of his spacesuit and handed Grissom a corned beef sandwich. Grissom said, "I took a bite, but crumbs of rye bread started floating all around the cabin so I stowed the rest of it."[3] After learning about the sandwich caper, NASA officials were very angry. Crumbs could have gotten into the instruments and created a serious safety hazard.

At the end of three orbits, Grissom fired the retro-rockets that would slow the spaceship out of orbit and return it to Earth. There was an unexpected jolt when the main parachute was deployed. Gus Grissom said, "John and I were both thrown against the windshield. I banged into a knob that punctured a hole in my face plate. John's face plate was only scratched. Then we were in the water."[4]

Molly Brown went down in the Atlantic, sixty miles from the rescue ship, the U.S.S. *Intrepid*. The still-attached parachute blew across the water and towed the capsule behind it underwater. Grissom quickly threw the switches to release the parachute and the spacecraft rose to the surface, where it floated like a cork. Grissom, remembering the near disaster aboard *Liberty Bell 7*, did not open the hatch.

Since the U.S.S. *Intrepid* was sixty miles away, it took the rescue team about thirty minutes to get to *Molly Brown*. During that time it got hot in the bobbing

One of the astronauts is lifted by a helicopter after splashing down in the Atlantic Ocean. A flotation collar kept the capsule afloat after the hatch was opened.

capsule, so the astronauts took off their spacesuits. Both men were feeling seasick by the time the Navy divers attached a flotation collar and the hatch was opened. In their long underwear, Grissom and Young were hoisted aboard a hovering helicopter and taken to a rescue ship full of cheering sailors.

After the successful flight of *Molly Brown*, Project Gemini continued to pile up success after success. Ed White made the first United States space walk during the *Gemini 4* mission. On *Gemini 8*, Neil Armstrong and David Scott performed the first docking between two spacecraft.

That mission almost ended in disaster. After *Gemini 8* and the Agena target rocket were locked together, both began to tumble through space. Unlocking the Agena only made the capsule spin faster and faster. An almost unconscious Neil Armstrong finally brought the capsule under control by blasting away on the nose rocket thrusters for thirty minutes.

Following Neil Armstrong and David Scott's near disaster, four more missions were flown in the Gemini program. During each of the twelve Gemini missions, new information was learned that would allow NASA to land a man on the Moon. It was during these years that America not only caught up with the Soviet space program, but passed it.

With the end of Project Gemini, NASA was ready to shoot for the Moon with the Apollo program. Gus Grissom was selected to fly aboard the first Apollo mission, along with Edward White and Roger Chaffee.

5

Destination: The Moon

With its eyes on a Moon landing, NASA stepped up the pace in its brand-new headquarters in Houston. Formally opened in 1964, the Manned Space Center contained dozens of buildings that were separated by winding pathways. New neighborhoods nearby housed the hundreds of MSC employees and their families. Gus and Betty Grissom, along with their sons, Mark and Scott, moved into a new house near the space center in 1964. With training facilities now located at MSC, Gus Grissom could spend more time with his family.

Gus Grissom and his crew on *Apollo 1* were not scheduled to fly to the Moon. As the first flight in the new program, they would only orbit Earth to test the spacecraft. Still, the astronauts spent hundreds of hours practicing procedures. They had to know just how to react in case of an emergency.

As time drew near for the February 1967 launch of *Apollo 1*, a Saturn rocket was moved to launchpad 34 at Cape Canaveral. Atop the rocket was the Apollo Command Module, which was twelve feet high and nearly thirteen feet at the base. Inside the capsule were three reclining seats for the crew, hundreds of dials and switches, and fifteen miles of wiring.

Just before noon on January 27, 1967, the three-man crew of *Apollo 1* ate lunch and then suited up for a

Gus Grissom and his crew needed many hours of training with the new Apollo spacecraft before they could test it in space.

The crew of Apollo 1 consisted of (left to right) Virgil I. Grissom, Edward H. White II, and Roger B. Chaffee. The crew was announced about a year before the scheduled flight.

simulation of the countdown that would take place in a month. After the men were in the cabin, the hatch was closed and sealed from the outside. Ninety seconds were needed to reopen the hatch from the inside. The cabin was filled with pure oxygen and pressurized, just as it would be before an actual launch.

The men strapped themselves into their seats. Chaffee was on the right, with White in the middle, and Grissom on the left. The simulation began at 1:00 P.M. Eastern Standard Time and went on all afternoon. During the hours of the test, the crew sometimes could not hear transmissions from the control center because of static. Gus Grissom said, "If I can't talk with you only five miles away, how can we talk to you from the Moon?"[1]

After five hours of testing, one engineer in the control center said, "Let's cancel out today. This could go on forever."[2] Instead of quitting for the day, Skip Chauvin, the spacecraft test conductor, started the countdown again at 6:31 P.M. In the blockhouse on the ground, NASA officials and technicians monitored the flight data and watched the astronauts on closed-circuit television monitors.

At T minus ten minutes in the countdown, astronaut Ed White suddenly shouted, "Fire!" Then Gus Grissom said, "I've got a fire in the cockpit!"[3] In the blockhouse, everyone froze and watched in horror as the capsule interior erupted in a flash of fire. The pad crew, who were up on the gantry, or framework, that held the Apollo capsule, grabbed fire extinguishers and ran to get the hatch open. The men were driven back by an explosion that ripped through the spacecraft and blasted smoke and flames out of the side of the command module.

Finally, six minutes after the fire flashed, the ground crew pried the hatch open. One worker said, "You wouldn't want a description of what we found in there."[4] Astronaut Deke Slayton later said,

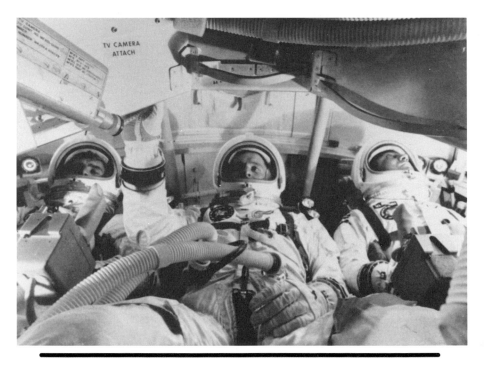

The television camera in the upper left corner sent images of the astronauts—(left to right) White, Chaffee, and Grissom—to Mission Control during the simulated launch.

It was devastating. Everything inside was burned, black with ash. It was a death chamber. The crew had obviously been trying to get out. The three bodies were piled in front of the seal in the hatch. Ed White was on the bottom and Gus and Roger were crumpled on top of him.[5]

The men themselves were not burned. Their spacesuits protected them from the flames. Because of the pure oxygen atmosphere in the cabin, everything flammable burned with super intensity and produced toxic fumes. The men suffocated when those fumes contaminated their air supply. The astronaut's bodies remained in the burned-out capsule for more than seven hours as NASA technicians investigated the disaster. At 12:55 A.M., the bodies of forty-year-old Gus Grissom, thirty-six-year-old Edward White, and thirty-one-year-old Roger Chaffee were finally removed from the charred cabin of *Apollo 1*.

6

Epilogue

On February 10, 1967, Gus Grissom was buried with full military honors at Arlington National Cemetery, located near Washington, D.C. President Lyndon Johnson sat with Betty Grissom and her sons, Mark, age thirteen, and Scott, age sixteen. Nearby, the remaining six Mercury astronauts stood at attention for their fallen comrade while jets thundered in the sky overhead and rifle shots rang in the cold, clear air.

Roger Chaffee was also buried at Arlington later in the day, in a grave next to Gus Grissom. Edward White was buried at the United States Military Academy, on a bluff overlooking the Hudson River in New York. President Johnson said that the "three valiant young men have given their lives in the nation's service."[1]

Soon after the funerals, a board of inquiry was convened to investigate the lethal fire aboard the thirty-five-million-dollar *Apollo 1* spacecraft. In a report submitted on April 5, 1967, the Review Board concluded that the fire started when a wire short-circuited near Gus Grissom's seat. The panel said that "the *Apollo 1* atmosphere was lethal 24 seconds after the fire had started and that consciousness was lost between 15 and 30 seconds after the first suit failed."[2]

Continuation of the Apollo program was delayed while NASA engineers examined every possible reason

Virgil I. "Gus" Grissom is buried at Arlington National Cemetery.

for the fire. The cabin hatch was redesigned so that it could be opened in seconds from inside, instead of the minute and a half needed to get the old hatch open. Also, the pure oxygen atmosphere in the cabin was changed to one of mixed gases. Pure oxygen fed a fire much too well, as the tragedy aboard *Apollo 1* demonstrated.

It would be twenty-one months before another manned Apollo mission lifted off. During the nearly two years between *Apollo 1* and *Apollo 7*, three unmanned flights were flown to test the huge Saturn V rocket and the Lunar Module. Complicated docking and rendezvous maneuvers between the Command Module and Lunar Module were also tested and refined. On October 11, 1968, *Apollo 7* was launched from Cape Canaveral. It was followed by nine more manned missions in the Apollo program. During the flight of *Apollo 11*, America landed its first astronauts on the Moon. Except for the near disaster aboard *Apollo 13*, all of the flights were successful and there were no more fatalities.

Several weeks before his tragic death, Gus Grissom said, "If we die, we want people to accept it. We're in a risky business, and we hope if anything happens to us, it will not delay the program."[3]

CHRONOLOGY

1926—Gus Grissom born on April 3 in Mitchell, Indiana.

1944—Graduated from high school.

1945—Married Betty Moore on July 6.

1950—Graduated from Purdue University; joined Air Force.

1951—Awarded Air Force wings.

1955—Sent to test-pilot school at Edwards Air Force Base.

1957—*Sputnik 1* launched by Soviet Union on October 4.

1958—National Aeronautics and Space Administration (NASA) created.

1959—Grissom among the first seven United States astronauts selected.

1961—Russian cosmonaut Yuri Gagarin became first person to fly in space aboard *Vostok 1* on April 12; Alan Shepard became first American to fly in space aboard *Freedom 7* on May 5; Grissom became second American to fly in space aboard *Liberty Bell 7* on July 21.

1964—The Grissom family moved to Houston, the site of the new NASA headquarters.

1965—Grissom flew aboard *Molly Brown*, the first two-man Gemini flight, on March 23.

1967—Gus Grissom, Edward White, and Roger Chaffee died in a fire on January 27 during a simulation of *Apollo 1* launch; Gus Grissom buried with full military honors at Arlington National Cemetery on February 10.

CHAPTER NOTES

Chapter 1

1. "Swimming Grissom Snatched Up by 'Copter' as Capsule Sinks in Sea," *Houston Chronicle,* July 21, 1961, p. A1.

2. "A-Okay—Almost All the Way," *Newsweek,* July 31, 1961, p. 19.

3. Ibid., p. 20.

4. "Saga of Liberty Bell," *Time,* July 28, 1961, p. 35.

5. Ibid.

6. Ibid.

7. "A-Okay—Almost All the Way," p. 21.

Chapter 2

1. "Saga of Liberty Bell," *Time,* July 28, 1961, p. 34.

2. Alan Shepard and Deke Slayton, *Moon Shot* (Atlanta: Turner Publishing Company, 1994), p. 38.

3. Ibid., p. 65.

4. Ibid., p. 62.

5. "Saga of Liberty Bell," p. 34.

Chapter 3

1. "Put Them High on the List of Men Who Count," *Life,* February 3, 1967, p. 25.

2. Alan Shepard and Deke Slayton, *Moon Shot* (Atlanta: Turner Publishing Company, 1994), p. 98.

3. Edgar Cortright, *Apollo Expeditions to the Moon* (Washington, D.C.: National Aeronautics and Space Administration, 1975), p. 18.

Chapter 4

1. Dick Lattimer, *All We Did Was Fly to the Moon* (Gainesville, Fla.: The Whispering Eagle Press, 1985), p. 46.

2. Gus Grissom and John Young, "Molly Brown Was OK From the First Time We Met Her," *Life,* April 2, 1965, p. 42.

3. Ibid.

4. Ibid.

Chapter 5

1. Alan Shepard and Deke Slayton, *Moon Shot* (Atlanta: Turner Publishing Company, 1994), p. 198.

2. Ibid.

3. Ibid., p. 201.

4. "Fire in the Spacecraft," *Newsweek,* February 6, 1967, p. 27.

5. Shepard and Slayton, p. 207.

Chapter 6

1. Al Rossiter, Jr., "3 Apollo Astronauts Meet Death Sealed in Blazing Space Capsule," *Houston Chronicle,* January 28, 1967, p. A1.

2. Dick Lattimer, *All We Did Was Fly to the Moon* (Gainesville, Fla.: The Whispering Eagle Press, 1985), p. 47.

3. Ibid., p. 46.

GLOSSARY

altitude—Height above sea level.

blockhouse—A building that serves as an observation point for an event that will involve a blast or heat hazard.

cosmonaut—A Russian astronaut.

debriefing—Recounting the details of a flight after it has taken place.

gantry—Framework that holds the rocket and spacecraft in place before launch.

NASA—National Aeronautics and Space Administration, created in 1958.

orbit—The path of one celestial body or artificial satellite around another.

retro-rockets—Rockets fired to slow the spacecraft before reentry into Earth's atmosphere.

satellite—A smaller celestial body or object that orbits a larger one.

simulator—Model used for training that reproduces the conditions of an actual situation.

velocity—The speed of an object in a given direction.

zero gravity—The absence of gravitational force exerted on a body, which causes weightlessness.

FURTHER READING

Asimov, Isaac. *Piloted Space Flights.* Milwaukee: Gareth Stevens Publishing, 1990.

Cole, Michael D. *Apollo 13: Space Emergency.* Springfield, N.J.: Enslow Publishers, Inc., 1995.

Mullane, Mike. *Liftoff.* Englewood Cliffs, N.J.: Silver Burdett Press, 1995.

Neal, Valerie, Cathleen Lewis, and Frank Winter. *Spaceflight: A Smithsonian Guide.* New York: Prentice Hall, 1995.

Ride, Sally. *To Space and Back.* New York: Lothrop, Lee & Shepard Books, 1986.

Shepard, Alan, and Deke Slayton. *Moon Shot.* Atlanta: Turner Publishing Company, 1994.

Wolfe, Tom. *The Right Stuff.* New York: Farrar, Straus & Giroux, Inc., 1979.

INDEX